Let us make friends with our bodies,
once and for all.

www.rosewoman.com

Special discounts are available on quantity purchases by corporations, associations, and others. For details, contact the publisher at the address above.

Publisher's Cataloging-in-Publication data

Author: Christine Marie Mason

Illustrator: Maria Rozalia Finna (Ouvra)

Designer: Colleen Shelley

Body Love: A Companion Journal to The Invitation

ISBN-13: 978-0-9977277-9-1

1. SELF-HELP / Journaling
2. SELF-HELP / Eating Disorders & Body Image
3. SELF-HELP / Personal Growth / Self-Esteem

FIRST EDITION

*This content is not intended to be a substitute for professional medical advice, diagnosis, or treatment. Always seek the advice of your physician or other qualified health provider with any questions you may have regarding a medical condition.

Introduction

This is our one body in this lifetime. It's an amazing vehicle for fun, love, play, service—everything we do. We've imbibed so many stories on how to be, how to look. But what if we just dropped them, stopped apologizing, looked at these bodies with love, and invited freedom? Loving our bodies is like any habit or muscle, it gets stronger with practice. That's what this journal is meant to help with. Changing the stories and living at peace with this magnificent organism of us.

Ways to show the body love

On the upcoming journal pages, you'll see a little checklist of suggestions on how to show your body love on a daily basis. There are also blank boxes for you to write in your answers. You might add other boxes for other actions and rituals—like "doing my physical therapy exercises," or even highly targeted interventions like "massaging the scar tissue on my knee."

It's our perspective that humans are incarnate spirits, woven of consciousness and energy. While we have a permanent consciousness (or "soul") that isn't anchored to the body, we are living in a body. Our bodies' health responds to our thoughts, as well as to the thoughts of the collective culture. When those thoughts are negative, they can limit our freedom and happiness.

We're here to tell you that those beliefs can be unwound. The Body Love Journaling, and the suggested self care practices in the checklists, are designed to support a reintegration: a restitching together of the body, mind, and spirit.

In addition to these exercises, questions are sprinkled throughout the book. They were created to help you evoke and examine the cultural beliefs that you've inherited about your body. They are questions about sex, shape, size, function, illness, and aging. About who your body belongs to, and who can make decisions about it. About what it can eat or drink or ingest. About what medical procedures are allowed and disallowed—even about how your body should be dressed. We ask things like: "Is your body here to please others?" "How is a body's quality related to a person's worth?" Our hope is that, upon examination, there are some beliefs you might like to leave behind forever!

For thousands of years, women's bodies have been under the control of others. Our sexuality has been controlled to regulate reproduction (largely to manage transgenerational wealth, but I won't go into that here—you can read about that elsewhere, which I hope you do!). But you know that there is a deep split within culture. We celebrate our animal selves by idealizing, decorating, fetishizing, optimizing, improving, and being encouraged to sexualize our bodies. At the same time, many religions and societies have shamed behaviors like dancing, exposing any part of the body, carnality (literally fleshiness), and sex in general. Women are told to hide their skin, while at the same time drawing power from being sexual. They are told to not be too fat or too skinny, and to be fashionable, yet at the same time are shamed for being shallow if they are overly in thrall to outward beauty standards.

What we wish for, in every person, is a new ability to see and feel your beautiful body from the inside—instead of from the outside, which is a kind of self-objectification. I wish for you to really inhabit your body, with love. When we take care of our bodies, this is a natural extension of our love; not intended to get anywhere or make our body "better," but to be present and appreciative of what we have.

Getting in the habit of loving your body can include a lot of practical things. The checklists we put in the Body Love Journal suggest:

Talking to it with kindness

Appreciation or gratitude practice can be a helpful way to change our dialogue with our body. There's a proactive way of doing this: we thank each part of the body for its function and service, and stand in awe of the trillion cooperating cells that make it work. We include this in our anointing practice as well: moving from head to toe, while noticing and feeling and thanking the body. There's also a reactive way of doing this: Anytime a criticism arises, cancel it out with a threefold praise (example: the thought arises, "my thighs are too big." Then you self correct: "Uh, uh, no you don't—these beautiful legs let me run, lift, carry the world. These legs take me everywhere I want to go. These legs are miracles of form and function."). *Reprogram your mind.*

Feeding it healthfully and beautifully

In the "lowering the body load" section of *The Invitation*, we talk about taking the stress off of your body systems. One way to do this is by avoiding foods that require a lot of energy to digest and process. The closer you can get to a vegetable, fruit, nut, and seed-based diet, along with organic animal products (if you take those in), the easier it is on your body.

We say "beautifully" because taking the time to arrange your food, plate it, and eat it in a nice setting is part of fully experiencing a meal. Blood types, constitutions, culture, time, and taste buds all contribute to what we eat. So make it a practice to ask: *If I was eating in order to feel great, what choices would I make?*

Drybrushing

This is an excellent all over practice which helps clean out debris and toxins in the body and boost immune function. Using a dry bristle brush, brush the skin of the upper torso toward the lymph nodes in the armpits, then brush the skin of the lower torso toward the lymph nodes in the groin. A video on our YouTube channel demonstrates how to do this.

Breathing deeply

Breathing is, generally speaking, automatic: The brain stem controls the rate of breathing in response to blood-oxygen levels, as measured by receptors in the aorta. These blood-oxygen levels change in response to demands made by other systems in the body. If you break into a run, for example, the demand for blood oxygen immediately increases, causing you to breathe faster.

Breathing controls heart rate, blood pressure, digestion, excretion, and absorption. Breathwork—voluntary control of the breath—is an entry point to our personal control of the autonomic nervous system. It helps us override physical, conditioned responses to perceived threats. By controlling our breathing, we bring the autonomic nervous system and its related glandular and hormonal triggers back into balance. Respiration is, in fact, the only system of the ANS over which we have control. Breathwork positively improves immune function, hypertension, asthma, autonomic nervous system imbalances, and psychological or stress-related disorders. It also alters the brain's information processing, improving our psychological functioning.

In addition to deep, slow breathing—even just 5 minutes of it— there are various breathing exercises you can do to recalibrate and balance the nervous system when it needs calming, activating, etc. You can find demonstrations of these exercises on our blog or YouTube channel.

Anointing

Once, trekking through a small Nepali village, I greeted several mothers who were sitting on the packed-earth steps outside their homes. Each was holding a naked baby or a small child, and massaging it from head to toe with oil. The babies cooed with pleasure. The image stayed with me, partly because the casual ritual seemed so similar to ones I'd seen being performed at Hindu weddings and other ceremonies, during worship of embodiments of gods and goddesses. These mothers were not just applying oil— they were blessing with touch, and transmitting a message of love, respect, and communion. They were nourishing a connection. To nourish in this way is the essence of anointing.

A self-anointing practice goes like this: After bathing, in the morning, start at your toes and give yourself a reverent foot-to-crown self massage. Coupled with affirmations, this can have a remarkable effect on the body-mind. Our skin is by far our largest organ, with the miraculous ability to absorb sunlight, moisture, essential oils, balms, and even vitamins. We have the ability to nourish (or harm, so only use pure products!) our skin directly through the unguents we apply. To anoint ourselves (and our babies, and our lovers) shows a high form of reverence for life.

Taking supplements

We're big fans of food as first medicine—and also of high quality supplements. People often begin a regimen of taking supplements, but lose the habit. We include this on the list as a reminder that this is another way to love yourself. Whatever your body is needing, take the time to support it—with supplements ranging from probiotics to Vitamin C, from adrenal support to CBD.

Dancing and/or Exercising

Vigorous movement practice, getting full mobility in all your joints, firing your muscles, trying new activities, putting some stress on your system so it gets stronger and more agile—these are all ways to love yourself.

Hydrating

Drinking adequate fluids enhances digestion, skin, brain function and more.

Resting

Indulge your body in sleep and spaciousness around activities. These might include bedtime rituals—like going to sleep at the same time every night, turning off your phone and (any blue light devices) an hour before bed, oxytocin-generating activities like touch or masturbation; all of these things can improve sleep. Your meditation practice and a full day off weekly can introduce the body to a rhythm of taking breaks.

Playing

Unstructured time to crawl, jump, play tag, make believe, explore. We love this quote from Hunter S. Thompson:

"Life should not be a journey to the grave with the intention of arriving safely in a pretty and well preserved body, but rather to skid in broadside in a cloud of smoke, thoroughly used up, totally worn out, and loudly proclaiming 'Wow! What a Ride!'"

Receiving touch

In yoga, it's often harder for people to receive the inhale than to exhale. Similarly, it's harder for some people to take in complements than to give them. For this self care practice, allow someone to give you asexual but loving touch, with no intention or obligation to reciprocate. Just receive. Let yourself be loved.

Sitting in silence

Of all the things on this list, taking time each day to be alone with yourself, to access the humming presence of all creation, with a mind stilled by practice or meditation, is probably the most important exercise on the list. It feeds and supports all the other practices. Aim for 15 minutes to start with, and see what happens as you sit. You may find you naturally want more and more time in this delicious free space. If you're not a meditator, if your mind runs away on you, if sitting with yourself in the quiet initially brings up an anxiety that you should be *doing something*... know that you're not alone. These are normal reactions as the busy, ever-doing mind struggles to assert control! But as you sit and breathe and turn inward, slowly you will have moments of total peace. These will ripple into your entire life as a stable, loving, non-reactive presence. Many free meditation resources are available as apps, streams, videos, classes, and more, all over the web and in every language.

Being outside

We're designed to live in the air and wind and rain and sunshine. The Norwegians have a saying: *"There's no bad weather, only bad clothing."* Being in nature—especially around oceans, waterfalls, and other places where ions are released from crashing water, or in the forest or woods, where you are in hyperoxygenated air, breathing with the trees—is super beneficial. A little sunshine and Vitamin D goes a long way. If you live in a city, get yourself into a park or a garden, and be with the growing things.

Giving it sensory pleasure

All of your six senses can be activated as forms of self love. Working with beautiful music, flowers, candles, a comfortable chair—all are much more pleasurable than bad posture in a messy, noisy room. Tantra teaches us to pay exquisite attention to our senses. It's a way of deeply appreciating the incredible details of our given reality. Bathing, touch, and self massage also fall into this category. Even dressing the body beautifully can contribute to sensory pleasure!

Giving it sexual pleasure

Sexual arousal and orgasm are good for you. Lovemaking and self pleasuring are some of the best ways to live happily in a body. There are many resources online for supporting a happy, healthy, engaged sexual and sensual life, from the onset of menses to old age. More resources than ever are going into eliminating pain, trauma, or difficulty in sexuality. Being sexually active is not a mandate; about 1% of the population is asexual by nature. But should you want sexual fulfillment as part of your life, it is yours for the taking.

The checklists in the book are meant to draw your
attention to the idea that body love is not abstract—
it is the direct result of applied actions.

An Example of a
Self Anointing Practice

5 to 20 minutes a day

- Start at the toes and work upwards

- Rub and massage in varying ways: light finger brushing for lymphatic massage; kneading for improved circulation and muscle relaxation; pulling skin from muscle over fascia, scars and lumpy tissues; deep and pressure points for sore areas, caressing for gentle loving touch.

- At each body part, say thank you — the more specific you are with your appreciations, the better. For example, "thank you feet, that feel the grass; thank you calves, that allow me to stand on my toes; thank you ribcage, that protects me. Include your vulva, rear, anus, and breasts. Work all the way up to the ears.

- Sample anointment mantra goes like this. "Thank you, I love you, I will listen to you and I will care for you, you are perfect."

- A longer affirmation might go like this, "My body is nature. My body is made perfectly in harmony with sun and air and food and water. Thank you body, for giving me so many experiences and sensations." or "Life wants itself and is expressing through me in this body. In this body, I create and serve and reflect a completely unique view of creation. Thank you body."

- No person or thing thrives in criticism. If any negative self talk arises around that body part, just notice and release it. This is the way your body is made right now, give it unconditional love. Over time this negative talk will diminish.

To complete:

- Express some gratitude for life and stay in silence for a few moments, while the body absorbs the oil and the love.

- Pass the loving kindness on to someone else energetically, thinking of someone who needs space and time and touch and kindness

Journal

How did I relate to my body today?

I showed my body love today by:

☐ Talking to it with kindness	☐ Taking supplements	☐ Receiving touch
☐ Feeding it healthfully and beautifully	☐ Dancing and/or Exercising	☐ Sitting in silence
☐ Drybrushing	☐ Hydrating	☐ Being outside
☐ Breathing deeply	☐ Resting	☐ Giving it sensory pleasure
☐ Anointing	☐ Playing	☐ Giving it sexual pleasure
☐	☐	☐
☐	☐	☐

The chance of you being born at all is 1 in 400 trillicn.
This life is a precious incarnation.

DATE: _________________   LOCATION: ___________________________

How did I relate to my body today?

I showed my body love today by:

☐ Talking to it with kindness	☐ Taking supplements	☐ Receiving touch
☐ Feeding it healthfully and beaut fully	☐ Dancing and/or Exercising	☐ Sitting in silence
☐ Drybrushing	☐ Hydrating	☐ Being outside
☐ Breathing deeply	☐ Resting	☐ Giving it sensory pleasure
☐ Anointing	☐ Playing	☐ Giving it sexual pleasure
☐	☐	☐
☐	☐	☐

Taking the time to practice awareness, inquiry, silence,
gratitude is a gift not only to yourself, but to everyone you
encounter and to the world at large. So thank you!
Thank you for journaling today.

How did I relate to my body today?

I showed my body love today by:

☐ Talking to it with kindness	☐ Taking supplements	☐ Receiving touch
☐ Feeding it healthfully and beautifully	☐ Dancing and/or Exercising	☐ Sitting in silence
☐ Drybrushing	☐ Hydrating	☐ Being outside
☐ Breathing deeply	☐ Resting	☐ Giving it sensory pleasure
☐ Anointing	☐ Playing	☐ Giving it sexual pleasure
☐	☐	☐
☐	☐	☐

"Body shame is absolutely contagious, and so is radical self-love.
We get to decide which one we're going to spread."

- SONYA RENEE TAYLOR

How did I relate to my body today?

I showed my body love today by:

☐ Talking to it with kindness   ☐ Taking supplements   ☐ Receiving touch

☐ Feeding it healthfully   ☐ Dancing and/or   ☐ Sitting in silence
  and beautifully   Exercising   ☐ Being outside

☐ Drybrushing   ☐ Hydrating   ☐ Giving it sensory
                                                                  pleasure
☐ Breathing deeply   ☐ Resting

☐ Anointing   ☐ Playing   ☐ Giving it sexual pleasure

☐   ☐   ☐

☐   ☐   ☐

If you are getting activated by the same things over
and over, there's something to investigate: it's a pointer
to a place where more freedom may be possible.

How did I relate to my body today?

I showed my body love today by:

- ☐ Talking to it with kindness
- ☐ Feeding it healthfully and beautfully
- ☐ Drybrushing
- ☐ Breathing deeply
- ☐ Anointing
- ☐
- ☐

- ☐ Taking supplements
- ☐ Dancing and/or Exercising
- ☐ Hydrating
- ☐ Resting
- ☐ Playing
- ☐
- ☐

- ☐ Receiving touch
- ☐ Sitting in silence
- ☐ Being outside
- ☐ Giving it sensory pleasure
- ☐ Giving it sexual pleasure
- ☐
- ☐

"Body Peace is the confidence and strength we possess when we trust our body's natural wisdom and beauty and draw on this trust to develop a healthy, flourishing life. Body Peace is a type of Power that allow us to feel confident with ourselves and our place in the world."

- SHELLY PRUITT JOHNSON

How did I relate to my body today?

<table>
<tr><td colspan="3" align="center">I showed my body love today by:</td></tr>
<tr>
<td>☐ Talking to it with kindness</td>
<td>☐ Taking supplements</td>
<td>☐ Receiving touch</td>
</tr>
<tr>
<td>☐ Feeding it healthfully and beautifully</td>
<td>☐ Dancing and/or Exercising</td>
<td>☐ Sitting in silence</td>
</tr>
<tr>
<td>☐ Drybrushing</td>
<td>☐ Hydrating</td>
<td>☐ Being outside</td>
</tr>
<tr>
<td>☐ Breathing deeply</td>
<td>☐ Resting</td>
<td>☐ Giving it sensory pleasure</td>
</tr>
<tr>
<td>☐ Anointing</td>
<td>☐ Playing</td>
<td>☐ Giving it sexual pleasure</td>
</tr>
<tr>
<td>☐</td>
<td>☐</td>
<td>☐</td>
</tr>
<tr>
<td>☐</td>
<td>☐</td>
<td>☐</td>
</tr>
</table>

What is considered "beautiful" changes with the times, but your actual beauty does not. What were you told was a "beautiful" body? Has that not changed even in your lifetime? Who wants their joy to be dependent on what's in fashion?

How did I relate to my body today?

I showed my body love today by:

☐ Talking to it with kindness	☐ Taking supplements	☐ Receiving touch
☐ Feeding it healthfully and beautifully	☐ Dancing and/or Exercising	☐ Sitting in silence
☐ Drybrushing	☐ Hydrating	☐ Being outside
☐ Breathing deeply	☐ Resting	☐ Giving it sensory pleasure
☐ Anointing	☐ Playing	☐ Giving it sexual pleasure
☐	☐	☐
☐	☐	☐

How did I relate to my body today?

I showed my body love today by:

☐ Talking to t with kindness	☐ Taking supplements	☐ Receiving touch
☐ Feeding it healthfully and beautifully	☐ Dancing and/or Exercising	☐ Sitting in silence
☐ Drybrushing	☐ Hydrating	☐ Being outside
☐ Breathing deeply	☐ Resting	☐ Giving it sensory pleasure
☐ Anointing	☐ Playing	☐ Giving it sexual pleasure
☐	☐	☐
☐	☐	☐

Sometimes even the things we get compliments on are a sort of prison, shaping our behavior. Do the things you get compliments on support the part of you that is emergent and true?

How did I relate to my body today?

I showed my body love today by:

☐ Talking to it with kindness	☐ Taking supplements	☐ Receiving touch
☐ Feeding it healthfully and beautifully	☐ Dancing and/or Exercising	☐ Sitting in silence
☐ Drybrushing	☐ Hydrating	☐ Being outside
☐ Breathing deeply	☐ Resting	☐ Giving it sensory pleasure
☐ Anointing	☐ Playing	☐ Giving it sexual pleasure
☐	☐	☐
☐	☐	☐

"If you're pretty, you're pretty; but the only way to be beautiful is to be loving. Otherwise, it's just 'congratulations about your face'."

- JOHN MAYER

How did I relate to my body today?

<hr>

I showed my body love today by:

☐ Talking to it with kindness	☐ Taking supplements	☐ Receiving touch
☐ Feeding it healthfully and beautfully	☐ Dancing and/or Exercising	☐ Sitting in silence
☐ Drybrushing	☐ Hydrating	☐ Being outside
☐ Breathing deeply	☐ Resting	☐ Giving it sensory pleasure
☐ Anointing	☐ Playing	☐ Giving it sexual pleasure
☐	☐	☐
☐	☐	☐

"Where did I get that belief? Who taught me that?
Who profits off of my self-loathing? Who does well because I feel
terrible about myself? Is it true? Do I personally, objectively,
believe it? Can I choose not to believe it anymore?"

- SONYA RENEE TAYLOR

How did I relate to my body today?

<table>
<tr><td colspan="3" align="center">I showed my body love today by:</td></tr>
<tr>
<td>☐ Talking to it with kindness</td>
<td>☐ Taking supplements</td>
<td>☐ Receiving touch</td>
</tr>
<tr>
<td>☐ Feeding it healthfully
　 and beaut fully</td>
<td>☐ Dancing and/or
　 Exercising</td>
<td>☐ Sitting in silence</td>
</tr>
<tr>
<td>☐ Drybrushing</td>
<td>☐ Hydrating</td>
<td>☐ Being outside</td>
</tr>
<tr>
<td>☐ Breathing deeply</td>
<td>☐ Resting</td>
<td>☐ Giving it sensory
　 pleasure</td>
</tr>
<tr>
<td>☐ Anointing</td>
<td>☐ Playing</td>
<td>☐ Giving it sexual pleasure</td>
</tr>
<tr>
<td>☐</td>
<td>☐</td>
<td>☐</td>
</tr>
<tr>
<td>☐</td>
<td>☐</td>
<td>☐</td>
</tr>
</table>

"Our culture is a punishment ethos, meaning that we base a lot of
our decisions on how to avoid pain or how to avoid discomfort.
Instead, we can start asking ourselves 'What feels good for me?'"

- DR. CAT MEYER

How did I relate to my body today?

<table>
<tr><td colspan="3" align="center">I showed my body love today by:</td></tr>
<tr>
<td>☐ Talking to it with kindness</td>
<td>☐ Taking supplements</td>
<td>☐ Receiving touch</td>
</tr>
<tr>
<td>☐ Feeding it healthfully and beautifully</td>
<td>☐ Dancing and/or Exercising</td>
<td>☐ Sitting in silence</td>
</tr>
<tr>
<td>☐ Drybrushing</td>
<td>☐ Hydrating</td>
<td>☐ Being outside</td>
</tr>
<tr>
<td>☐ Breathing deeply</td>
<td>☐ Resting</td>
<td>☐ Giving it sensory pleasure</td>
</tr>
<tr>
<td>☐ Anointing</td>
<td>☐ Playing</td>
<td>☐ Giving it sexual pleasure</td>
</tr>
<tr>
<td>☐</td>
<td>☐</td>
<td>☐</td>
</tr>
<tr>
<td>☐</td>
<td>☐</td>
<td>☐</td>
</tr>
</table>

How did I relate to my body today?

I showed my body love today by:

☐ Talking to t with kindness   ☐ Taking supplements   ☐ Receiving touch

☐ Feeding it healthfully
and beautifully   ☐ Dancing and/or
Exercising   ☐ Sitting in silence

☐ Being outside

☐ Drybrushing   ☐ Hydrating   ☐ Giving it sensory
pleasure

☐ Breathing deeply   ☐ Resting

☐ Anointing   ☐ Playing   ☐ Giving it sexual pleasure

☐   ☐   ☐

☐   ☐   ☐

"People are so impressed with an app or a machine. But think about life itself: an infinite, self evolving, self reproducing thing that contains all of a species history, and all of its future. This complexity and perfection is beyond human comprehension. The only answer is wonder and awe."

- CHRISTINE MARIE MASON

How did I relate to my body today?

I showed my body love today by:

☐ Talking to it with kindness	☐ Taking supplements	☐ Receiving touch
☐ Feeding it healthfully and beaut fully	☐ Dancing and/or Exercising	☐ Sitting in silence
☐ Drybrushing	☐ Hydrating	☐ Being outside
☐ Breathing deeply	☐ Resting	☐ Giving it sensory pleasure
☐ Anointing	☐ Playing	☐ Giving it sexual pleasure
☐	☐	☐
☐	☐	☐

"I could be wrong" is an invitation to the self to break
a patterned belief. What might I be wrong about today?

How did I relate to my body today?

I showed my body love today by:

☐ Talking to it with kindness   ☐ Taking supplements   ☐ Receiving touch

☐ Feeding it healthfully and beautifully   ☐ Dancing and/or Exercising   ☐ Sitting in silence

☐ Drybrushing   ☐ Hydrating   ☐ Being outside

☐ Breathing deeply   ☐ Resting   ☐ Giving it sensory pleasure

☐ Anointing   ☐ Playing   ☐ Giving it sexual pleasure

☐   ☐   ☐

☐   ☐   ☐

When are you most alive, happy, at peace?

How did I relate to my body today?

I showed my body love today by:

☐ Talking to it with kindness   ☐ Taking supplements   ☐ Receiving touch

☐ Feeding it healthfully and beautifully   ☐ Dancing and/or Exercising   ☐ Sitting in silence

☐ Drybrushing   ☐ Hydrating   ☐ Being outside

☐ Breathing deeply   ☐ Resting   ☐ Giving it sensory pleasure

☐ Anointing   ☐ Playing   ☐ Giving it sexual pleasure

☐   ☐   ☐

☐   ☐   ☐

“Where are you vulnerable? What soothes you?
Can you self-soothe or do you lean on others to regulate you?”

– DR. CAT MEYER

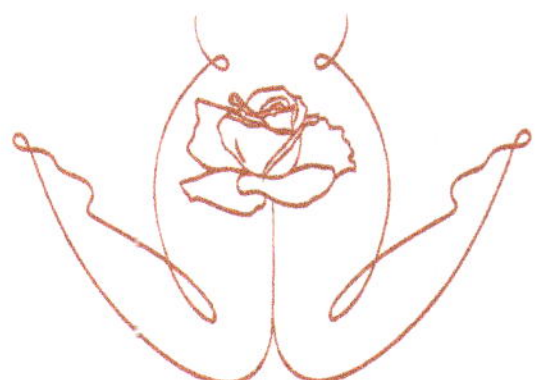

DATE: _________________   LOCATION: _________________

How did I relate to my body today?

I showed my body love today by:

- ☐ Talking to t with kindness
- ☐ Feeding it healthfully and beautifully
- ☐ Drybrushing
- ☐ Breathing deeply
- ☐ Anointing
- ☐
- ☐

- ☐ Taking supplements
- ☐ Dancing and/or Exercising
- ☐ Hydrating
- ☐ Resting
- ☐ Playing
- ☐
- ☐

- ☐ Receiving touch
- ☐ Sitting in silence
- ☐ Being outside
- ☐ Giving it sensory pleasure
- ☐ Giving it sexual pleasure
- ☐
- ☐

How did I relate to my body today?

I showed my body love today by:

☐ Talking to it with kindness	☐ Taking supplements	☐ Receiving touch
☐ Feeding it healthfully and beautifully	☐ Dancing and/or Exercising	☐ Sitting in silence
☐ Drybrushing	☐ Hydrating	☐ Being outside
☐ Breathing deeply	☐ Resting	☐ Giving it sensory pleasure
☐ Anointing	☐ Playing	☐ Giving it sexual pleasure
☐	☐	☐
☐	☐	☐

"Hiding from sight is a byproduct of shame—but we don't
have to come out all at once. Just give yourself a little bit more
freedom every day and watch how it accumulates."

-CHRISTINE MARIE MASON

How did I relate to my body today?

I showed my body love today by:

☐ Talking to it with kindness	☐ Taking supplements	☐ Receiving touch
☐ Feeding it healthfully and beautifully	☐ Dancing and/or Exercising	☐ Sitting in silence
☐ Drybrushing	☐ Hydrating	☐ Being outside
☐ Breathing deeply	☐ Resting	☐ Giving it sensory pleasure
☐ Anointing	☐ Playing	☐ Giving it sexual pleasure
☐	☐	☐
☐	☐	☐

"We are all of our ages at once."

-CHRISTINE MARIE MASON

How did I relate to my body today?

I showed my body love today by:

☐ Talking to it with kindness   ☐ Taking supplements   ☐ Receiving touch

☐ Feeding it healthfully and beautifully   ☐ Dancing and/or Exercising   ☐ Sitting in silence

☐ Being outside

☐ Drybrushing   ☐ Hydrating   ☐ Giving it sensory pleasure

☐ Breathing deeply   ☐ Resting

☐ Anointing   ☐ Playing   ☐ Giving it sexual pleasure

☐   ☐   ☐

☐   ☐   ☐

When does your body feel best?

How did I relate to my body today?

I showed my body love today by:

☐ Talking to it with kindness

☐ Feeding it healthfully and beautifully

☐ Drybrushing

☐ Breathing deeply

☐ Anointing

☐

☐

☐ Taking supplements

☐ Dancing and/or Exercising

☐ Hydrating

☐ Resting

☐ Playing

☐

☐

☐ Receiving touch

☐ Sitting in silence

☐ Being outside

☐ Giving it sensory pleasure

☐ Giving it sexual pleasure

☐

☐

What could you let go of right now to find a little more freedom?

How did I relate to my body today?

I showed my body love today by:

☐ Talking to it with kindness ☐ Taking supplements ☐ Receiving touch

☐ Feeding it healthfully and beautifully ☐ Dancing and/or Exercising ☐ Sitting in silence

☐ Being outside

☐ Drybrushing ☐ Hydrating ☐ Giving it sensory pleasure

☐ Breathing deeply ☐ Resting

☐ Anointing ☐ Playing ☐ Giving it sexual pleasure

☐ ☐ ☐

☐ ☐ ☐

Waiting for life to begin is a habit of mind: when I get fit,
when I get wealthy, then I will be happy. Are there any
"waiting for" or "putting off" patterns at work in my life?

How did I relate to my body today?

I showed my body love today by:

☐ Talking to it with kindness   ☐ Taking supplements   ☐ Receiving touch

☐ Feeding it healthfully
and beautifully   ☐ Dancing and/or
Exercising   ☐ Sitting in silence

☐ Being outside

☐ Drybrushing   ☐ Hydrating   ☐ Giving it sensory
pleasure

☐ Breathing deeply   ☐ Resting

☐ Anointing   ☐ Playing   ☐ Giving it sexual pleasure

☐   ☐   ☐

☐   ☐   ☐

How did I relate to my body today?

I showed my body love today by:

☐ Talking to it with kindness	☐ Taking supplements	☐ Receiving touch
☐ Feeding it healthfully and beautfully	☐ Dancing and/or Exercising	☐ Sitting in silence
☐ Drybrushing	☐ Hydrating	☐ Being outside
☐ Breathing deeply	☐ Resting	☐ Giving it sensory pleasure
☐ Anointing	☐ Playing	☐ Giving it sexual pleasure
☐	☐	☐
☐	☐	☐

"Our words have magic, they are incantations, literally enchanting the mind. Thoughts precede emotions, which precede actions. When we change our language, we change the way we feel, and slowly, our lives begin to change."

-CHRISTINE MARIE MASON

How did I relate to my body today?

I showed my body love today by:

- ☐ Talking to it with kindness
- ☐ Feeding it healthfully and beautifully
- ☐ Drybrushing
- ☐ Breathing deeply
- ☐ Anointing
- ☐
- ☐

- ☐ Taking supplements
- ☐ Dancing and/or Exercising
- ☐ Hydrating
- ☐ Resting
- ☐ Playing
- ☐
- ☐

- ☐ Receiving touch
- ☐ Sitting in silence
- ☐ Being outside
- ☐ Giving it sensory pleasure
- ☐ Giving it sexual pleasure
- ☐
- ☐

"Love is the through line, it connects us to the source
of life and to each other, it animates our life and work.
In all we do and say, let our love be our fuel."

-CHRISTINE MARIE MASON

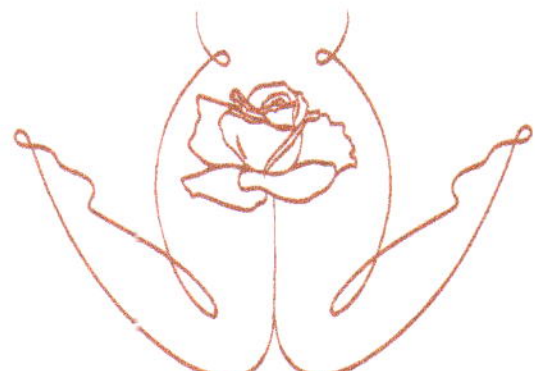

DATE: _________________________   LOCATION: _________________________________

How did I relate to my body today?

What did you learn about sex and sexuality in your
formative years? Which of those ideas are helpful and
true and which do you want to leave in history?

How did I relate to my body today?

I showed my body love today by:

☐ Talking to it with kindness   ☐ Taking supplements   ☐ Receiving touch

☐ Feeding it healthfully   ☐ Dancing and/or   ☐ Sitting in silence
   and beautifully   Exercising
                                                  ☐ Being outside

☐ Drybrushing   ☐ Hydrating   ☐ Giving it sensory
                                                      pleasure

☐ Breathing deeply   ☐ Resting

☐ Anointing   ☐ Playing   ☐ Giving it sexual pleasure

☐   ☐   ☐

☐   ☐   ☐

What did you learn about the shape and size of bodies, especially
your body, in your formative years? Which of those ideas are
helpful and true and which do you want to leave in history?

How did I relate to my body today?

I showed my body love today by:

☐ Talking to t with kindness	☐ Taking supplements	☐ Receiving touch
☐ Feeding it healthfully and beautifully	☐ Dancing and/or Exercising	☐ Sitting in silence
☐ Drybrushing	☐ Hydrating	☐ Being outside
☐ Breathing deeply	☐ Resting	☐ Giving it sensory pleasure
☐ Anointing	☐ Playing	☐ Giving it sexual pleasure
☐	☐	☐
☐	☐	☐

What did you learn about health and illness and capacity
of your body in your formative years? Which of those ideas are
helpful and true and which do you want to leave in history?

71

How did I relate to my body today?

I showed my body love today by:

☐ Talking to it with kindness	☐ Taking supplements	☐ Receiving touch
☐ Feeding it healthfully and beautifully	☐ Dancing and/or Exercising	☐ Sitting in silence
☐ Drybrushing	☐ Hydrating	☐ Being outside
☐ Breathing deeply	☐ Resting	☐ Giving it sensory pleasure
☐ Anointing	☐ Playing	☐ Giving it sexual pleasure
☐	☐	☐
☐	☐	☐

What did you learn about aging as a woman in your formative years? Which of those ideas are helpful and true and which do you want to leave in history?

How did I relate to my body today?

I showed my body love today by:

☐ Talking to it with kindness	☐ Taking supplements	☐ Receiving touch
☐ Feeding it healthfully and beautifully	☐ Dancing and/or Exercising	☐ Sitting in silence
☐ Drybrushing	☐ Hydrating	☐ Being outside
☐ Breathing deeply	☐ Resting	☐ Giving it sensory pleasure
☐ Anointing	☐ Playing	☐ Giving it sexual pleasure
☐	☐	☐
☐	☐	☐

Who does your body belong to and who can make decisions about it?

How did I relate to my body today?

I showed my body love today by:

☐ Talking to it with kindness
☐ Feeding it healthfully and beautifully
☐ Drybrushing
☐ Breathing deeply
☐ Anointing
☐
☐

☐ Taking supplements
☐ Dancing and/or Exercising
☐ Hydrating
☐ Resting
☐ Playing
☐
☐

☐ Receiving touch
☐ Sitting in silence
☐ Being outside
☐ Giving it sensory pleasure
☐ Giving it sexual pleasure
☐
☐

How did I relate to my body today?

I showed my body love today by:

☐ Talking to it with kindness

☐ Feeding it healthfully and beautifully

☐ Drybrushing

☐ Breathing deeply

☐ Anointing

☐

☐

☐ Taking supplements

☐ Dancing and/or Exercising

☐ Hydrating

☐ Resting

☐ Playing

☐

☐

☐ Receiving touch

☐ Sitting in silence

☐ Being outside

☐ Giving it sensory pleasure

☐ Giving it sexual pleasure

☐

☐

Is your body here to please others? What have you been
taught, and what do you want to carry forward?

How did I relate to my body today?

I showed my body love today by:

☐ Talking to it with kindness	☐ Taking supplements	☐ Receiving touch
☐ Feeding it healthfully and beaut fully	☐ Dancing and/or Exercising	☐ Sitting in silence
☐ Drybrushing	☐ Hydrating	☐ Being outside
☐ Breathing deeply	☐ Resting	☐ Giving it sensory pleasure
☐ Anointing	☐ Playing	☐ Giving it sexual pleasure
☐	☐	☐
☐	☐	☐

How did I relate to my body today?

I showed my body love today by:

☐ Talking to it with kindness	☐ Taking supplements	☐ Receiving touch
☐ Feeding it healthfully and beautifully	☐ Dancing and/or Exercising	☐ Sitting in silence
☐ Drybrushing	☐ Hydrating	☐ Being outside
☐ Breathing deeply	☐ Resting	☐ Giving it sensory pleasure
☐ Anointing	☐ Playing	☐ Giving it sexual pleasure
☐	☐	☐
☐	☐	☐

"In times of stress, our greatest friend is our breath.
It's the only part of our nervous system that we can consciously
override. Big, round, slow deep breaths are medicine."

-CHRISTINE MARIE MASON

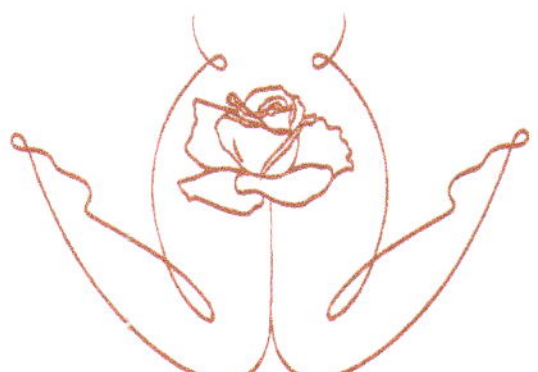

How did I relate to my body today?

I showed my body love today by:

☐ Talking to it with kindness	☐ Taking supplements	☐ Receiving touch
☐ Feeding it healthfully and beautifully	☐ Dancing and/or Exercising	☐ Sitting in silence
☐ Drybrushing	☐ Hydrating	☐ Being outside
☐ Breathing deeply	☐ Resting	☐ Giving it sensory pleasure
☐ Anointing	☐ Playing	☐ Giving it sexual pleasure
☐	☐	☐
☐	☐	☐

We're operating on multiple developmental levels at once—
can you tell when you're responding to the world from a
young place and from a wise adult place?

How did I relate to my body today?

I showed my body love today by:

☐ Talking to it with kindness	☐ Taking supplements	☐ Receiving touch
☐ Feeding it healthfully and beautifully	☐ Dancing and/or Exercising	☐ Sitting in silence
☐ Drybrushing	☐ Hydrating	☐ Being outside
☐ Breathing deeply	☐ Resting	☐ Giving it sensory pleasure
☐ Anointing	☐ Playing	☐ Giving it sexual pleasure
☐	☐	☐
☐	☐	☐

I love eating! It's one of life's great sensory pleasures. I reclaim all tastes and nourishments as wholly available to me. Nothing is off limits. How could your relationship with food be more of a celebration?

How did I relate to my body today?

I showed my body love today by:

☐ Talking to it with kindness	☐ Taking supplements	☐ Receiving touch
☐ Feeding it healthfully and beautifully	☐ Dancing and/or Exercising	☐ Sitting in silence
☐ Drybrushing	☐ Hydrating	☐ Being outside
☐ Breathing deeply	☐ Resting	☐ Giving it sensory pleasure
☐ Anointing	☐ Playing	☐ Giving it sexual pleasure
☐	☐	☐
☐	☐	☐

"Girl, put your records on, play me your favorite song,
go ahead let your hair down..."

- CORINNE BAILEY RAE

How did I relate to my body today?

I showed my body love today by:

☐ Talking to it with kindness

☐ Feeding it healthfully and beautifully

☐ Drybrushing

☐ Breathing deeply

☐ Anointing

☐

☐

☐ Taking supplements

☐ Dancing and/or Exercising

☐ Hydrating

☐ Resting

☐ Playing

☐

☐

☐ Receiving touch

☐ Sitting in silence

☐ Being outside

☐ Giving it sensory pleasure

☐ Giving it sexual pleasure

☐

☐

"You're not 30 or 50 or 80: Your body is hundreds of thousands of years old. It contains all the evolved wisdom and experience of every generation before it."

– T. HUEBL

How did I relate to my body today?

I showed my body love today by:

☐ Talking to it with kindness	☐ Taking supplements	☐ Receiving touch
☐ Feeding it healthfully and beaut fully	☐ Dancing and/or Exercising	☐ Sitting in silence
☐ Drybrushing	☐ Hydrating	☐ Being outside
☐ Breathing deeply	☐ Resting	☐ Giving it sensory pleasure
☐ Anointing	☐ Playing	☐ Giving it sexual pleasure
☐	☐	☐
☐	☐	☐

Were you ever told to "contain yourself"—that ycu
were too much? Too much color? Too loud, too big?
If yes, what would it feel like to drop that story?

93

How did I relate to my body today?

I showed my body love today by:

- ☐ Talking to it with kindness
- ☐ Feeding it healthfully and beautifully
- ☐ Drybrushing
- ☐ Breathing deeply
- ☐ Anointing
- ☐
- ☐

- ☐ Taking supplements
- ☐ Dancing and/or Exercising
- ☐ Hydrating
- ☐ Resting
- ☐ Playing
- ☐
- ☐

- ☐ Receiving touch
- ☐ Sitting in silence
- ☐ Being outside
- ☐ Giving it sensory pleasure
- ☐ Giving it sexual pleasure
- ☐
- ☐

The mind wants to see the dangers and risks, but there are always hundreds of other things going on at the same time. This flower over here, the way the light reflects, the love of a friend, these are all just as real and present.

How did I relate to my body today?

I showed my body love today by:

☐ Talking to it with kindness　　☐ Taking supplements　　☐ Receiving touch

☐ Feeding it healthfully and beautifully　　☐ Dancing and/or Exercising　　☐ Sitting in silence

☐ Being outside

☐ Drybrushing　　☐ Hydrating　　☐ Giving it sensory pleasure

☐ Breathing deeply　　☐ Resting

☐ Anointing　　☐ Playing　　☐ Giving it sexual pleasure

☐　　☐　　☐

☐　　☐　　☐

If all of the frosting is stripped away, the makeup, or clothes that
we use to cover and shine and costume, how do we feel then
about our bodies and faces? Can we love ourselves unadorned?

How did I relate to my body today?

I showed my body love today by:

☐ Talking tc it with kindness	☐ Taking supplements	☐ Receiving touch
☐ Feeding it healthfully and beautifully	☐ Dancing and/or Exercising	☐ Sitting in silence
☐ Drybrushing	☐ Hydrating	☐ Being outside
☐ Breathing deeply	☐ Resting	☐ Giving it sensory pleasure
☐ Anointing	☐ Playing	☐ Giving it sexual pleasure
☐	☐	☐
☐	☐	☐

What would it take to be free, to respond in the moment to what's arising, without closing our hearts? To keep releasing the past and meet the world as it is now?

Reflection

Noticing changes over time

How did these practices influenced my relationship with my body? It's helpful to take a moment to see how doing these practices for 6 weeks have impacted you. These pages are meant for open ended reflection.

105

Closing exercise

Write a letter to your 13 year old self.
What would you want her to know about her body?

CLOSING EXERCISE

CLOSING EXERCISE

True wellness is about being free in mind, body and spirit.
We are each an agent of transformation. Let us pass on our
freedom and wisdom, not our suffering.

CPSIA information can be obtained
at www.ICGtesting.com
Printed in the USA
LVHW021916090420
652828LV00015B/18